CONTENTS

CW00859835

1

Jokes & Stories
One Liners

Longer

Introduction

The purpose of this guide is to share my own personal experience in overcoming the 'Having to Make a Speech ' hurdle.
The content is based on some more than a 100 occasions over years with both the Cornwall County Bowling Association, and Masonic Lodge activity where I had to make speeches or reply.

With a little thought the actual speeches that follow, although in all probability suffer from correct grammatical phraseology, can be adapted for most occasions. The Stories although not new can be used verbatim and will cause a certain amount of laughter and well being.
Let me say that I had very little experience in making speeches of any kind, and was always very nervous.
Grown men can be reduced to a near state of panic, and even the most normally erudite can become tongue tied, and hesitant
I therefore decided to follow the example set by Her Majesty The Queen, and many leading politicians, that is to

Prepare a Script and Read It

Believe me it really does work, removing all the um's and ah's, also the need to learn and commit the content to memory. Even if you manage this, it surprising how ones mind can go blank when in the 'Hot Spot'

Essential 'What Too Do' & 'What Not Too Do'

1. Gather as much relevant information as you can before
    Preparing your script, write and rewrite until you are satisfied
    It all hangs together.
2   What ever means you, use be it typewriter, word processor ,
    computer or handwriting (Preferably Block Capitals) make
    sure the print is sufficiently large to be able to read it clearly
    when held to read about waistline.height.
    I recommend the paper size to be no larger than 4 x 5 inches,
    It is not so obtrusive, and it looks as though you are holding a few
    notes rather than a prepared speech.
    Double spacing is an option to accommodate any last minute
    alterations than be necessary, but it does double the number of
    pages.

3   There are normally a certain number of formalities that must
    be included, if it is necessary to mention names, make sure that you
    do not miss anyone of importance.
4   Leave spaces in your text for entering the VIP names in your
    address.
    One does not normally know who they are until the actual event.
5   Select one or two stories suitable for the occasion, but make a
    note of which you told where.
    It saves repeating a story to the same people, although a good
    story will always go down well with those that have heard it
    Before.

5   Practice reading your script aloud, preferably standing until
    Your speech sounds just like the normal way you converse
    On a face to face basis.
    If you are softly spoken you will need to practice throwing
    your voice, as you will often be in large premises, and the people at
    the back want to hear what you have to say as well as anyone else
    present.
    It is important to sound perfectly natural. Get someone to listen
    and make constructive comment, not on the content, but on
    the presentation.
    Time your speech, short entertaining speeches are appreciated
    more than long boring ones.
6   One major benefit of having a prepared speech in your pocket
    Is that you can relax and enjoy your meal with the company that
    you are seated with, confident in what you are going to say, rather
    than what is often the case without a script, a loss of appetite and
    awareness of what is going on around, all that one
    Can think of is the time when you are expected to stand up and face
    the music.
7   When you are introduced, stand up and smile all round, and
    Remember it is common courtesy to thank who ever has introduced
    you.
    When you stand, it is of no importance whether you just push your
    chair back, or whether you stand behind it.
    Basic principle Stand Up, Speak Up, Shut Up and Sit Down

Weddings
The Best Man

I have always failed to understand why the Bridegrooms right hand man is called 'The Best Man'

Surely it is the Bridegroom who is the Best Man, after all he is the one who has got married today, not me, and it is supposed to be my duty to look after him, and I am not sure who was more nervous in Church.

It was probably knowing that I had to bat first in the speeches stakes.

Did you know that apparently many generations ago if the bridegroom failed to turn up for the wedding, the best man had to take his place.

My other main duty today is to look after the Bridesmaids, and what a pleasant task that is, but first I must take this opportunity to wish ...... & .... A long and happy marriage, which is a sentiment shared by many others according to all these cards and telegrams. (Read the cards & Telegrams)

I congratulate the Bride on her appearance, she looks
a picture of health and beauty, just like all the delightful
young ladies she has chosen to be her Bridesmaids.

In time no doubt they will be brides themselves, and I wish them all, good health, good luck and every future happiness.

Ladies & Gentlemen

I ask you all to rise and join me in the traditional toast
' To The Bridesmaids'

Wedding
The Brides Father, Toast to The Bride & Groom

Today is another significant milestone in our family history, although I am afraid to say that at the last minute it nearly didn't happen, for just as we were leaving home, a woman driving one of those very large continental estate cars with about 14 kids on board ran a red traffic light and just stopped short of hitting us.

I was naturally a little upset at the thought of what could have happened, so I wound down and in a rather un gentlemanly manner shouted *'Can't you stop woman'* to which she quickly replied *'they are not all mine'*

Seriously on behalf of my Wife……. and myself it gives me great pleasure to formally welcome ……..to our family.

Although it has been said many times before we have not lost a daughter, but gained a son.

Marriage has often been likened to an institution, but as a very good friend of mine said *'Who the hell wants to live in an institution'*

Anecdotes proffered by old hands at the marriage game are legion here are a few:

"Marriage is like a bath, once you are in, it's not so hot."

" Marriage is the difference between painting the town, and painting the back porch."

A man is incomplete until he is married, then he is completely finished, but the one that I think typifies a good strong marriage is: Marriage resembles a pair of shears, joined together so they cannot be separated. Often moving in opposite directions, but woe betide anyone that comes between them.

If ……. & ……. Take heart and stand together shoulder to shoulder to face the ups and downs of every day life, they will enjoy a long and happy marriage.

It is my fondest hope that they will share every happiness and good health.

Ladies & Gentlemen please rise and let us wish our happy couple all the good luck in the world.

The Toast is " The Bride & Groom"   6

The Bridegroom

Mum, Dad, Family and Friends, as you will quickly see, I am not up to this speech making lark, which probably explains why I feel some what like a swan, serene on the surface, but paddling like hell underneath.

However on behalf of my Wife and I we thank you for sharing this happiest day of our lives.

Thank you ……………and …………..for undertaking the other speeches.

A very big thank you to both Mums and Dads for all they have done, not only for to day , but for all the years they have brought us up.

I hope that ……… and I can make as good a job of married life as they have, and that all our children will grow up as nice as my Wife.

We thank everyone for the excellent choice of wedding gifts, they will bring happy memories in the years to come.

Thanks to ………….. my best man for all his support, he has been a real tower of strength.

Thank you all for this lovely day, God Bless Everyone

Fraternal

The Initiate

Brother………….., we can all mark momentous occasions in our lives and one of the most significant is being admitted to the ancient and honourable fraternity of Freemasons.

It is my privilege and pleasure to welcome you to the craft in general and to the ………………..Lodge in particular.

This evening you are placed in a position of honour at the right hand of the Master. We trust that you in turn will honour us by striving to attain the Masonic knowledge necessary to eventually progress to the high office within our order .

I fully appreciate that what you have experienced today is probably not very clear to you, we have performed a ceremony of Initiation that is the foundation on which you may raise a superstructure on which by making a daily advancement in Masonic knowledge you will ultimately reflect honour to yourself and the craft.

Brethren please be upstanding and drink a bumper toast to 'The Initiate'.

(A response from the Initiate should preferably be spontaneous and short)

Toast to the Visitors

Worshipful Master, Brethren All

Over the years it has always slightly bothered me that we use the term Visitors rather than Guests, so I took a rare dive into a dictionary to discover that there is in fact no substantial difference so Brethren Welcome.

I could not begin to count the number of times this toast has been given up and down the country in craft lodges, so it would be impossible to say anything that has not been said before.

I do however believe that one of the most important facets that makes a successful Lodge is to ensure that visiting brethren enjoy being with us.

Here at .... Lodge we are proud of the hospitality we endeavour to extend, now although hospitality has been defined as the art of making people feel at home, when you wish they were, that most certainly does not apply here, for you are very welcome.

 Brethren we thank you for being with us today, we trust that you enjoyed the working in the temple and our festive board.

When you leave tonight have a safe journey as we wish to see you again.

Members of .... please rise and drink a bumper toast to the health of our Visitors.

Responding to the Visitors Toast

Worshipful Master & Brethren

I regret that I cannot list after dinner speaking as one of my major accomplishments.

This probably explains why I feel some what like a swan, serene on the surface but paddling like hell underneath.

On behalf of the visitors I congratulate the ……………..

Lodge for the manner in which the ceremony was performed.

The high standard is not attained without a lot of study, full marks to you all.

In studying one has to read, and the other day I saw an article in a popular magazine that referred to a Teacher admonishing a small boy in class for swearing.

" Billy you must not use language like that, where on earth did you hear it"

" My Dad says it" replied Billy

"That makes no difference, you must not use words like that, after all you do not even know what it means"

" Oh yes I do Miss, it means the car won't start"

Brethren of the ………………lodge, thank you for making us so welcome ,thank you for the splendid festive board we have thoroughly enjoyed our evening with you, and look forward to visiting again.

Thank you Brother ……..for the way that you proposed the Toast, and you brethren for the way you received it.

Ladies Festival, Toast to the Ladies

Mr President, Ladies and Gentlemen

It is an honour for me to be charged this evening with what we consider to be the most important toast of the year. To our Ladies. I regret that my limited ability in after dinner speech making does not do justice to the appreciation that our ladies so richly deserve. I may not be able to adequately extol their charms, but I can claim to be a devoted admirer, and may I say how perfectly charming you all look this evening.

Now the ladies festival is the annual occasion for the Men folk to say thank you for all the support and forbearance during the year. They say that behind every successful man there is a woman, and a particular thank you is due to our Presidents Lady for the support of our president during his very busy year of commitments.

Over recent years there has been quite a lot of discussion regarding the equality of women, as though it was something to be argued about, for it does not exist, women have never been equal, for they have always proved to be superior, and long may it continue, let the ladies remain as different, feminine, and irresistible as now.

Tonight could be considered a significant Anniversary for I am reminded of the couple celebrating their Golden Wedding.

On being interviewed by a local reporter in response to the question " How had they enjoyed their lives"

The Husband replied " We have been happily married all these years because I make all the big decisions, and my Wife makes all the small ones"

Asked what the small decisions were ? he replied " What we do generally, where we go on holiday, what we eat, who our friends are, who we invite to our house, when to go to bed, when we get up, and things like that"

" I see" said the reporter, what are the big decisions you make ?"

"Well, things like who will be the next president of the United States, the state of the economy, settling the problems in various countries around the world, who will lead the next Government.

Ladies on behalf of all the gentlemen present, we are delighted to see you, proud to be in your company and trust that you will enjoy a happy, enjoyable and memorable evening.

Gentlemen charge your glasses and be upstanding and join me in wishing continued health and happiness to our ladies.

The Toast " Our Ladies"   11

The Sports Scene
Home Game Welcoming the Visitors

President/ Chairman/Captain............... Gentlemen/Ladies

On behalf of .... it is my pleasure to extend a warm welcome to the members of ....

We are enjoying/have enjoyed the companionship so unique to our game, the score is irrelevant being a simple matter of arithmetic, something you would expect an Accountant to be quite adept at.

Well I knew of an accountant who replied to an advertisement for a top job with a large company.

On submitting his CV he was invited to an interview with the Chairman of the board, who right at the end said " Just one last question, what is 3 x 7.

The Accountant thought for a minute, and replied 22.

Outside the Chairman's office he took out his pocket calculator and realised the answer should have been 21.

He concluded that he had lost the job and was surprised to receive a letter a few days later offering him the post.

Having taken up the position, a few weeks passed when he asked the Chairman why he had been offered the job when he had given the wrong answer to the calculation.

The Chairman replied "Because you were the closest."

Gentlemen/Ladies please join me in thanking the Ladies/Caterers for the excellent buffet/tea/refreshment

Thank you all for your participation today, I wish you good health, good luck and a safe journey home.

Away Game
Response
President/Chairman/Captain……………….....Ladies/Gentlemen
The one thing on taking office in my Club/Association was the
thought of having to make speeches at matches and annual dinners,
but a very good friend gave me the following advice.
"Nothing to it" he said " You stand up, say a few thanks, tell a story
and sit down"
So President/Chairman/Captain I thank you for your warm
welcome, irrespective of the result of the game it was our intention
to enjoy the game and your company. This we have done and I
thank you for that and your excellent hospitality.
and would ask President/Chairman/Captain to pass our thanks for
the use of all the facilities to the Club Committee accordingly.
The Ladies have done us proud and we thank you for the excellent
buffet/tea/refreshment.
Thanks also to our respective Match Secretaries for making all the
necessary arrangements.

Umpires are an essential part of our game and I must tell you about
the devil continually challenging St Peter to a match.

St Peter always refused until one day he noticed that he could call
on quite a few international players that had recently passed
through the pearly gates. So he accepted the next challenge from
the Devil, who promptly said " You will definitely lose"

" I cannot see why you should be so confident" said St Peter
" After all I have quite a few internationals in my team"
" Never you mind" said the Devil " You may have all the
internationals, but I have got all the Umpires"

President/Chairman/Captain………………thank you for a super
day, and behalf of the …………….. Club I thank all the members
of your team for their hospitality and companionship, I wish you all
Good Health, Good Luck and every success in your future
endeavours.

Annual Luncheon/Dinner " The Guests"

Distinguished Guests, Ladies & Gentlemen

It is my pleasure to welcome you all here today/this evening and in particular *(Here list all the VIPs by name, if there is a large number dependent on your style & confidence you can make an aside at this point.*

E.G. "That was like reading the Queens Birthday Honours list" or " Can I sit down now"

You can acknowledge each VIP with a little information about their role in the Association.

I would firstly like to thank all the members of the committee for all their hard work in ensuring that all the members of ……………
have enjoyed the year, and in particular…….

If you must identify individuals be careful not to leave any one out.

I would now crave the indulgence of our Guests for a few moments while I attend to one or two domestic matters, I pay tribute to……………….. *(List members who attained significant attainments during the year)*

Congratulations to all the Trophy Winners and I call upon……………. To assist in presenting the awards.

Now I am told that the art of good speaking is to tie any story you wish to tell to the context of what has gone before, unfortunately I cannot, so I crave your indulgence whilst I tell you of a little gem that I found in a popular monthly magazine.

When the creator was making the world he told man that he was giving him 20 years of normal sex life.

Man was unhappy about this and requested more. This was refused.
The monkey was offered 20 years also, but turned down 10 of them
Man pleaded for these extra ten, this time the creator graciously agreed.

The noble lion was offered 20 years and since he only wanted ten, the surplus was granted to man.

The Donkey was also offered 20 years , but said ten was enough.
Man again begged for the surplus and was granted a further ten more years.

This probably why man has 20 years of normal sex life, 10 years monkeying around, 10 years lion about it and 10 years making an ass of himself.

Members of ………………..please be upstanding and drink a toast to our Guests and the …………….Association.   14

Stories

Short
Corkscrew
One of our younger Club members had an unfortunate incident recently, he had to call the Doctor late at night to come urgently as apparently the baby had swallowed a corkscrew.

Five minutes later just as the Doctor had got dressed he received another call.

" Glad that I have caught you Doctor, sorry to have disturbed you, but everything is OK now, we have found another corkscrew.

County Library
Communication from County Hall to all local Authorities just before the end of the cold war.

In the event of nuclear attack the County libraries will manned by a skeleton staff.

Cream
Cream always rises to the top, and you all know what happens when you leave it standing around for a while.

Flea
A flea went into a bar, ordered one scotch after another, then hopped unsteadily out on to the pavement, leapt high in the air and fell flat on his face.

" Dammit" he said " Someone has moved my dog"

Hospitality
Hospitality has been defined as the art of making people feel at home, when you wished they were.

The Hunter
A Hunter was out with his gun, as he approached a wood a young lady ran out completely naked.

The Hunter said " are you game"

"Yes" she replied, so he shot her.

Short Stories Continued

Introduction
The Speaker slowly rose from his chair, drew himself to full height, and waited for the rapturous applause to die down.
An air of expectancy prevailed as the audience prepared to be entertained by an undoubted master of the craft.
What a shame you have got me.

No Change
Note to Headmaster
"Sorry Robert will not be at school today. I am keeping him in bed as he has swallowed a 50p piece.
I am calling the Doctor if there is no change by Monday.

Nursery Rhyme
There was an old lady that lived in a shoe, she had so many children she did'nt know what to do.......presumably

Recession
A time when we may have to do without things that our Grandparents have never heard of.

Trafficators
My local garage is run by an Irishman, to whom I took my car to recently to check the trafficators, he came out to have a look.
It's working, no it's not, yes it is, no it's not, yes it is

Wit
I was asked recently if you had to be a wit to hold high office.
"No" I replied, but I was probably only half right.

Longer Stories
Accident

I nearly didn't make it here tonight, for just as I was leaving home a woman driving one of those very large continental estate cars with about 14 kids on board ran a red traffic light, and just stopped short of hitting me.

I was naturally a little upset at the thought of what could have happened, so I wound my window down, and in rather un-gentlemanly manner shouted " Can't you stop women." To which she quickly replied " They are not all mine"

Accountant

As far as the game today we are, and I hope that you are also enjoying the companionship that is unique to our sport,
 score is irrelevant being purely a matter of arithmetic. Something you would expect accountants to be quite adept at.

I know of an accountant who applied for a top post with a large company.

His application brought him to an interview with the CEO, who at the end of the interview said " One last question what is 3 x 7 ? "
The Accountant thought for a minute and replied "22"
Outside he took out his pocket calculator and realised the answer should have been 21.

He concluded that he had lost the job, and was more than surprised to receive a letter a few days later offering him the post.
A few weeks passed having accepted the position when he asked the CEO why he had been appointed when he had given the wrong answer to the final question.
The CEO replied " Because you were the closest."

Advice

On gaining Office I was given some sound advice from a distinguished Past Officer.
He said " There will be many occasions that you will have to stand and say a few words and I would advise that you always remember not only your ABC but XYZ as well"
" Oh I see" I said " And what may this ABC and XYZ ?"
" ABC stands for 'Always Be Confident' but most important is the XYZ Which stands for 'Always Examine Your Zip' "   17

Longer Stories Continued

Anniversary

Anniversaries are always significant, and I am reminded of the couple celebrating their Golden Wedding, on being interviewed by a local reporter and replying to the question how they had enjoyed their lives, the Husband replied " We have been happily married all these years because I make all the big decisions, and my Wife makes all the small ones.

Asked what the small decisions were he answered,

" What we do generally, where we go on holiday, what we eat, who we invite to the house, when to go to bed, when to get up and things like that "

" I see " said the reporter " What then are the big decisions that you make ?"

Well things like, who will be the next President of the United States, the state of the economy, settling the problems in the Middle East, and all matters concerning the United Nations

Bank Manager

The recent recessional times have hit most quite hard and small business has found it difficult to obtain support from banks.

Typical of the experience of a local small shopkeeper who on paying in at his local Bank requested to ask to see the Manager Mr Jones, The cashier replied " I am sorry but he died last week" " Oh " said the shop owner, who then left the Bank.

Three days passed and the shop owner went again to the Bank, Saw the same cashier, paid in and requested to see Mr Jones.

" I am sorry you cannot see Mr Jones as he passed away last week" " I see" said the shopkeeper, and went on his way.

At the end of the week he returned to the Bank, saw the same cashier, paid in and said " I would like to see the Manager Mr Jones"

The cashier very firmly said " I have already told you twice before that Mr Jones has died, can't you believe me ?"

Shopkeeper replied " Certainly I can, but I just like to hear you say it"

Bishops

Two Bishops stood at the gates of heaven, on being met by
St Peter they were requested to wait a few minutes.
Whilst waiting a very attractive blonde lady arrived, she was also
requested to wait, but whispered in St Peters ear, and was
immediately taken through the pearly gates.
The Bishops were a little upset at this preferential treatment, and
complained to St Peter, he replied " That woman's husband gave
her a brand new car some six months ago, during that time she put
the fear of God into more people than you have in the whole of
your lives"

Brothers

There were 11 brothers, the first was an Accountant, the second was
no good at figures either, the third was a Solicitor, the fourth was a
rogue also.
The fifth was a financier, the sixth was in a cell next to him, the
seventh won an OBE, the eighth had not seen any fighting either.
The ninth was a local man, the tenth had a funny accent as well,
while the eleventh was a bachelor…….Just like his father

Candlesticks

Apparently it is desirable when making a speech to link any story
with what you have just been talking about.
Unfortunately I can't, so I will tell you about the Bishop who had
received quite a few letters from local residents from one of his
parishes.

It would appear that their local curate had a far too attractive
House keeper.
The Bishop thought that there isn't any smoke without fire, so he
would visit the curate and stay for a day or two.
On arrival he was in no doubt that the housekeeper was most
certainly young and attractive.
All seemed in order, the Bishop could find no fault in the manner in
which the Curate behaved towards her.
During his stay he was taken on a conducted tour of the Parish and
the local Church, he was shown the highly prized and ornate solid
gold candlesticks what stood on the altar.   **(Continued)** 19

The Bishop took his leave and returned to his palace.

Three days later he received a letter from the Curate stating that the candlesticks were missing.

The Curate wrote " Of course I do not say that a man so eminent as your Grace has taken the candlesticks, but I think you will agree, that their disappearance on the day of your departure could be taken as strong circumstantial evidence.

The Bishop replied " My Son I do not accuse you of sleeping with your housekeeper, but you surely agree that the circumstantial evidence is very strong, you see that if you had slept in you own bed you would have found the candlesticks"

Cannibals

Father and Son were standing on the beach of a remote Pacific Island which was still notorious for indulging in occasional cannibalism.

They were watching the flotsam from a recent shipwreck, when a young scantily clothed blonde came stumbling towards the ashore. The son turned to his father saying " Shall I rush into the water, bring her ashore, take her home and we'll eat her.

Father being full of contemplative wisdom looked at the vision coming ashore and replied:

" No son rush into the water, bring her ashore, take her home and we'll eat your mother"

Cinema

Two men at the cinema were watching the huge figure of John Wayne approach the low door of a Mexican Taverna.

" Bet you a quid he bangs his head" said the first man."

"OK your on" replied the second man.

Sure enough he did bang his head, where upon the first man said " I've got to be honest I have seen this film before"

" So have I " replied the second man " But I didn't think he'd do it a second time"

Coal

Teacher gave the following problem during an arithmetic class.
If coal costs £3.00 a hundredweight how much coal would I get for
£30.
One small lad put his hand up, " Yes Billy" said the Teacher
" You would get 9cwts Miss"
Teacher shook her head " That's not right Billy"
" I know miss " said Billy " But they all do it"

Communication

A friend of mine spent part of a holiday on an Indian reservation,
this was at the time that nuclear testing was being undertaken in an
isolated part of the Nevada Desert.
One of the activities in the holiday was a field trip with an Indian
guide. Through out the day he regularly communicated with his
pals by smoke signals. Apparently there was quite an argument
taking place, for smoke signals were becoming fast and furious.
Suddenly there was an enormous explosion with a great mushroom
cloud billowing up to the heavens.
The Indian guide turned to my friend and said,
" I wish I had said that"

The Creator

When the creator was making the world he told man that he was
giving him 20 years of normal sex life.
Man was unhappy about this and asked for more.
The request was refused.
The monkey was offered 20 years also, but turned down 10 of
them.
Man pleaded for these extra ten, this time the creator graciously
agreed.
The noble lion was offered 20 years and since he only wanted ten,
the surplus was granted to man.
The Donkey was also offered 20 years , but said ten was enough.
Man again begged for the surplus and was granted a further ten
more years.
This probably why man has 20 years of normal sex life, 10 years
monkeying around, 10 years lyon about it and 10 years making an
ass of himself.

Cricket

Now you have heard it said many time that ……….. is a funny old game, but have you ever tried to explain cricket to an American.
It might go something like this. You have two sides, one out in the field, and one in. Each man that is in , in turn goes out, when he is out he comes in and the next man goes in until he is out.
When they are all out, the side that has been out in the field comes in and the side that has been in goes out, and tries to get those that come in out.
Then when both sides have been in and out including the not outs, that is the end of the game.

The Curate

A young curate moved into my area recently and decided to take up (Bowls, Golf etc) he came along to my club and introduced himself to the Secretary who directed him to join a young lady that had also just joined.
The curate had a speech impediment and introduced himself by saying " My name is pppp ..peter bbbbut I am no sssss..saint
The young lady had a speech impediment also, and replied
" Ppppleased to mmmmeet you, mmy nnname is mmmary,and I am not a vvver..very good (Bowler, Golfer)

Duke of Norfolk

The Duke of Norfolk is a keen supporter of National Hunt racing , and at a recent Aintree meeting he sent a string of runners accompanied by a party of stable lads and lassies to look after them. On the second day one of the stable lads was hauled before the local magistrates accused of indecent behaviour with one of the stable lasses apparently under the fence at Beechers Brook.
When asked " How do you plead ?" the stable lad replied
" Guilty as charged your honour, and I would like 16 other fences to be taken into account"

Elephants 1

A friend of mine recently returned from a coach holiday, you know the sort of thing drive 200/300 miles, stop overnight, up at 5.00 o'clock next morning and on the road again, and they call it a holiday.

During this particular holiday my friend sat next to a chap who was continually tearing up a newspaper into very small pieces and every few miles threw a handful out of the window.

My friends inquisitiveness got the better of him so he asked the fellow what was he doing ?

" Keeping the elephants away " he replied, but my friend said There are no elephants around here"

" I know" he said " Wonderfully effective isn't it"

Elephants 2

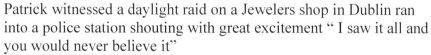

Patrick witnessed a daylight raid on a Jewelers shop in Dublin ran into a police station shouting with great excitement " I saw it all and you would never believe it"

" Believe what queried the desk Sergeant.

" Dammed great elephant lumbers down the street, smashes the window with his tusks, scoops all the jewels up with his trunk and makes off "

" Was it an Indian or African Elephant " the Sergeant asked.

"Don't know, how do you tell " said Paddy.

" Well Indian Elephants have small ears, while the African have large floppy ears ""What sort of ears did this one have ? "

"No idea " " Why not " " Because this one was wearing a stocking over its head "

Football,

The England Football teams chances for the world cup reminds me of when ex star Alan ball was asked what he thought the current side would fare against the 1966 World Cup Winning Team.

He thought for a moment, and said that he thought the 1966 team would beat the current side.

" By what score " he was asked. " Oh One Nil I would think"

" Why by such a small margin ?"

Alan thought again and said " You have to remember that we are now all over sixty"

Flag Poles

Did you hear about the Club that thought it was necessary to repaint their flagpole. The committee thought it prudent to obtain a quote first.

So a local firm sent two Irish painters along to measure up for a quote to be given.

Having forgotten their ladder, one climbed on the shoulders of the other to reach further up the pole.

The owner of the firm came along to see how they were getting on, and on seeing how they were tackling the job, said something like " Not like that you fools, undo the top bolt in the bottom bracket of the pole and lie it flat"

" Sorry Boss" said Paddy " I thought you asked to measure the height, you didn't say anything about the width"

Hong Kong Bowlers

World Bowls Tournament, Hong Kong player to an English International " Why is it that you English always seem to win the Singles Title, and we always lose?"

That's easy came the reply, because before we play an important game we pray.

"It can't be that" said the Hong Kong Bowler " For we always pray ourselves"

" Yes I know, but who the hell can understand Chinese ?"

Hospital

A local self employed JCB Driver was recently contracted by the Water Authority to dig a trench through the grounds of a mental hospital.

The Chief physiotherapist thought it would be beneficial to some of the inmates if they could assist.

Three were given shovels and told to report to the JCB Driver, he told them to square the sides at the bottom of the trench.

One promptly jumped into the trench, while the other two stood either side of the trench with their spades perfectly upright.

"That's no use " shouted the driver " Off you go, I don't need you"

Off they went immediately followed by the third inmate

" oi where do you think you are going " said the Driver.

" Sorry Boss I can't work without any light "

Jigsaw

Since the giving and receiving of presents are very much in mind at certain times of the year, I must tell you about paddy who went into his local and said to the barman " Drinks all round"

" What are we celebrating " said the barman

" I have just complete my jigsaw , and it only took 18 months.

" You took 18 months " said the barman, " That's hardly anything to celebrate" " Oh yes it is" said Paddy, " It says 3 to 5 years on the box"

Naval Officer

You have all heard some tall stories in the past, how about this, a young naval officer went down to the breakwater for a swim, he was just about to dive in, when a jellyfish spoke to him,

" I shouldn't go in there sir, it is very rocky, it is much better further along".

The officer thought a talking jelly fish was a little strange, so he engaged it in conversation.

The jellyfish explained that it was a long story, but to cut it short it was in fact a very attractive Wren who had been put under a magic spell.

The only way that the spell could be broken would be to put the jellyfish under some ones pillow at the bewitching hour, it would then be immediately turn back into a beautiful Wren.

The officer being only to willing to help, put the jellyfish into his pocket and returned to his ship.

At the bewitching hour he carefully placed the jellyfish on to his pillow. Unfortunately they didn't belief a word of it at his court marshal.

New Bowler

At one of the clubs we recently played against, one of the regular bowlers was unable to play, the club captain being a resourceful chap like most club captains, spotted a relatively new bowler who had turned up to watch, and said " Get you woods you're in"

" But I have only been playing for three weeks "

" That doesn't matter said the club captain, what position would you like to play".

" Well as I have only been playing a short time I had better go last".

Organisation

There are four main bones in any organisation.

The Wish Bones, wishing someone else would do something about the problem.

The Jaw Bones, who do all the talking and nothing much else.

The Knuckle Bones who seem to knock everything

And the Back Bones who carry the load and do most of the work.

Past President

I am not a great teller of stories but this could be appropriate.

Years ago I used to holiday on a farm in the Lake District.

I recall on one visit the farmer's dog had given birth to a litter of delightful puppies. They kept one and sold the rest., he was bright, alert, extremely keen, and always rushing around, so they named him Junior

The following year I revisited to find the puppy approaching maturity and undertaking some of the work around the farm, and proving to be quite an asset, so they had renamed him Senior.

Next year we found the dog to be fully grown and in complete command right on top of the job.

" What do you call him now " I enquired

" President " the farmer replied

It was some years before I could visit again, but in due course it happened to find that nothing much had changed, except there was an old grey tired looking, sheep dog lying in the corner of the farm yard.

Having been warmly greeted by the Farmer and his Wife after these several years, I enquired about the sheep dog that we were so impressed with on our last visit.

" I seem to recall that you called him President"

" Yes that's right " said the farmer " But we don't call him that now

" " What do you him now then ?"

" Past President" " Why do you call him that "

" Because all does now days is to sit on his backside & Yap

26

The Pope & The Umpires

When the last Pope died, and as you would expect he went to heaven. He was graciously received with due reverence by St Peter who conducted him to suitable lodgings, nothing ostentatious, but all very pleasant.

Having had a long journey the Pope retired early, and was awaked next morning by a tremendous noise. He went to the window to see the streets thronged with people, all cheering, and waving, ticker tape descending from adjoining buildings, a scene of great enthusiasm.

Coming down the street an open top limousine was slowly progressing, a figure stood in the back resplendent in red blazer and white flannels, raising his arms in acknowledgement of all the adulation.

At this moment St Peter knocked on the door and entered the Popes room.

The Pope by virtue of his calling was not given to pride or jealousy said to St Peter " Please do not think that I am complaining as my treatment has been most kind and considerate, but after all I was the Pope, and I am wondering what the fellow in the car has done to merit the reception he is receiving.

St Peter smiled and replied " Well you holiness, according to my records you are the 149th Pope, but that chap is our 1st County Umpire"

Schoolboy

The other day I saw an article in a popular magazine that referred to a Teacher admonishing a small boy in class for swearing.

" Billy you must not use language like that, where on earth did you hear it"

" My Dad says it" replied Billy

"That makes no difference, you must not use words like that, after all you do not even know what it means"

" Oh yes I do Miss, it means the car won't start"

Scotsman

Relying on a little ethnic humour, a Scottish lads first job took him south to London, his doting parents had arranged for him to live in a block of bachelor apartments.

His mother was very apprehensive of his ability to fend for himself for the first time in his life, so after a few weeks had passed she decided to take a trip to London to find out how he was getting on.
" How do you like living here son" she asked
" Och it's fine, except my neighbours, the idiot on this side keeps banging on the wall, while the one on the other side screams and yells most of the night".
" How on earth do you stand it laddie" queried his mother,
" What do you do while all this is going on ?"
" I don't do anything, I just carry on practicing on my bagpipes".

Signals

In a lot of sports verbal and visual signals appear to be a vital form of communication., the following signals were exchanged after a naval frigate collided with the admirals flagship.
Flag Officer to Captain of the Frigate
" What do you propose to do now ?"
Reply from Captain " Buy a Farm"

Shipwreck

A young businessman was looking to hire a bright Girl Friday and received so many applications he found the prospect of interviewing them quite daunting. He consulted a friend who worked in the personnel field for some guidance, which as a result enabled him to whittle the applicants down to just three.
He then asked how he would discover if they were of the right material, " That's easy " said his friend " Just ask each one what she would do if shipwrecked and swam to an island inhabited by only 40 men.
The interviews commenced, the question duly asked of the first young lady, she replied " I would swim away to another island"
The second thought that she would seek out the strongest man to protect her.
The third said " I heard the question, what's the problem"

Space

Apparently the Americans were considering sending a manned flight to Venus, but could not find anyone to undertake the mission, they decided to advertise and narrowed the applicants down to just three, an Italian, a Frenchman and an Israeli.

The Italian was examined first and found to be satisfactory on all counts, when asked what payment he required he replied " "One million Dollars"

The Frenchman was equally satisfactory but required two million dollars.

The Israeli was tested last and found to be perfectly satisfactory as well.

When asked how much he wanted, three million was the answer.

The Americans asked why three millions when the Italian will do the job for one million, and the Frenchman two million.

" It is quite simple " replied the Israeli there is a million for you, a million for me and we send the Italian.

24 Hours to Live

I heard of a man who was given just 24 hours to live by his doctor. He went home and broke the sad news to his wife who loyally planned to give him the perfect last few hours.

She suggested he played his last game of ......" no " he said

" Too many memories" " How about the theatre" she queried

" No" he replied " Not interested" " What about a meal at your favourite restaurant" " Couldn't face it " he said.

Getting desperate for ideas she decided to pass responsibility over to her husband, and asked him what he would like to do.

Without hesitation he replied " Take a case of champagne to bed and make love all night"

" That's all right for you" she replied " But you don't have to get up in the morning".

Unemployment

Recession has unfortunately led to an increase in unemployment, but I have found a solution to the problem.
You put all the men on one island, and all the women on another. That would soon make all the men gainfully employed.
Doing what you may ask ?
Boat building of course.

Umpires Bowls Match

An angel guarding the gates to heaven answered a knock on the door, there stood a man asking if he could come in.
"You are welcome" said the angel, but I would like to know whether you have performed any courageous act in you life, for without it you cannot enter.
" Yes I have " the man replied " My profession was ………….
But my hobby a Bowls Umpire.
" Indeed" Said the angel " And has this provided an opportunity for a courageous act.
Yes I was umpiring a match between ……….. & …………
Which had progressed to the final end all square. An extra end called for a measure to decide the outcome, there was a large contingent of supporters from both sides who awaited the result with bated breath. I carefully measured, re-measured and awarded the shot to ………….
" Well" said the angel" That was indeed a courageous act, providing that it can be verified ".
He then pressed his celestial telephone (Everyone keeps up with information technology these days) and spoke to records department requesting that the story be checked.
The answer came back that there was no record.
" Can you tell me when this happened ? " queried the angel.
The man looked at his watch and replied " Yes as a matter of fact it was 5 minutes ago".

Vicar & His Bicycle

One of our club members is a local vicar, have you noticed they all seem to ride bicycles, well this one was late for a match for apparently his bike had been stolen.

This prompted him on the following Sunday to give a sermon to his parishioners, not to simply obey 'Thou Shall Not Steal',

But to go through all of the ten commandments exhorting them to obey the rules to the letter.

After the service the curate congratulated him on his performance, but added that the vicar seemed to lose his way a little when he got to 'Thou shall not commit adultery'

" Yes sorry about that " said the vicar " But I suddenly remembered where I had left my bike"

The Virtuous Man

I am described by my friends as an exemplary man, I do not drink, I do not smoke, I do not go around with other women, I go to bed early, I get up early, I take exercise every day, and I do not get any financial reward whatsoever for this self denial.

Mind you it will all change as soon as I get out of prison.

Weight

These ……….teas have a lot to answer for when it comes to putting on weight, for believe it or not before I took this job on I weighed 13stone 2, now I have recently got up to the 16 stone mark.

Mind you I have no wish to get up to the weight of the chap that went to his doctor to seek advice on how to reduce from 19 stones.

" What is the least weight that you have ever weighed ? "

" 7lbs 6ozs " was the reply.

Witchcraft

Witchcraft is a practice that apparently still prevails in remote parts of Cornwall.

An eye witness reports that travelling down the North Coast On a dark rainy night last autumn, he saw a very attractive young lady thumbing a lift.

He stopped and picked her up, she was soaked to the skin and shivering. She was extremely grateful to get into the relative warmth of the car.

It subsequently transpired although young an attractive she was a witch.

The evidence being after travelling a mile or two engaging in conversation she accidentally or otherwise touched his knee,

Where upon he immediately turned into a lay by   31

4690991R00021

Printed in Germany
by Amazon Distribution
GmbH, Leipzig